Kick the Football, Charlie Brown!

LITTLE SIMON
An imprint of Simon & Schuster Children's Publishing Division
1230 Avenue of the Americas
New York, New York 10020
Manufactured in the United States of America
First Edition
2   4   6   8   10   9   7   5   3   1

Library of Congress Cataloging-in-Publication Data

Katschke, Judy.
Kick the football, Charlie Brown / adapted by Judy Katschke.—1st ed.
p. cm. — (Ready-to-read)
"Peanuts."
"Based on the comic strips by Charles M. Schulz."
Summary: Charlie Brown continues to try to kick the football and Lucy continues
to pull it away to make him fall down.
ISBN 0-689-84594-4 (alk. paper)
[1. Football—Fiction.] I. Schulz, Charles M. Peanuts. II. Title. III. Series.

PZ7.K15665 Ki 2001
[E]—dc21   2001035826

Kick the Football, Charlie Brown!

Based on the comic strips
by Charles M. Schulz
Adapted by Judy Katschke
Art adapted by Nick and Peter LoBianco

Little Simon
New York   London   Toronto   Sydney   Singapore

Happiness is a warm puppy!

Happiness is catching snowflakes
on your tongue!

Happiness is a side dish of french fries
with ketchup!

And sometimes . . . happiness is
kicking a football.

That's what Charlie Brown thought
when Lucy got a brand-new football.

"All you have to do is hold the ball, Lucy,"
Charlie Brown said.

"Then I'll come running up and kick it!"

Lucy held the football.

"I don't know if this is such a good idea," she said to herself.

Charlie Brown stepped back.

He charged toward the ball.

Then—Good grief! There *was* no ball!

Lucy had snatched it away!

What was the big idea?

"I was afraid your shoes might be dirty, Charlie Brown," Lucy said.

"I don't want anyone with dirty shoes kicking my football!"

Charlie Brown just rolled his eyes.

"Don't ever do that again!"
Charlie Brown warned Lucy.
"Do you want to kill me?
This time, hold it tight."
The next time Lucy *did* hold
the ball tight . . . too tight!

Charlie Brown stepped back.
He charged toward the ball.
He swung back his foot to kick.
Then—*THUMP!*
Charlie Brown landed on his big,
round head!
Again.

"I held it *real* tight, Charlie Brown!"
Lucy said with a smile.

Charlie Brown just stared up at the sky.

I'm never getting up, he thought.
I'm just going to lie here for the rest of the day.

The next day Lucy wanted Charlie
Brown to try again.

Charlie Brown said no.

"Oh, come on, Charlie Brown!"
Lucy pleaded.

"I'll hold it real steady."

"No!" said Charlie Brown.

"Please?" Lucy begged.

"No!" Charlie Brown said. "You just want me to come running up to kick that ball so you can pull it away and see me kill myself!"

Lucy looked Charlie Brown straight
in the eye.

"Just to show you I mean it, I'll give you a
million dollars if I pull the ball away!"

A million dollars? Charlie Brown gulped.

"In fact," Lucy said, "I'll give you one *hundred* million dollars!"

Charlie Brown gave it a thought. Lucy *had* to mean it if she was offering one hundred million dollars!

"I must be out of my mind," Charlie Brown told Lucy.

"But I can't resist kicking footballs."

Charlie Brown stepped back.
He charged toward the ball.
He swung back his foot to kick.

Then—"HA!" Lucy laughed
as she pulled the ball away.
WHAM! Charlie Brown's teeth rattled!

"Here's your money, Charlie Brown!"
Lucy joked.

She pretended to shower Charlie Brown
with dollar bills!

"Hee Hee Hee Hee Hee!" Lucy laughed
as she walked away.

"I think I'll lie here until it snows,"
Charlie Brown sighed.

Lucy balanced her football on the ground.

"Is that about right?" she asked Charlie Brown.

"Is that about right for what?" Charlie Brown asked.

"I'll hold the ball, Charlie Brown," Lucy said, "and you kick it!"

Charlie Brown couldn't believe his ears!
"Are you crazy?!" he shouted.
"You'll pull it away and I'll break my neck!
Do you think you can fool me with the same
stupid trick year after year after year?"

"But the odds are really in your favor, Charlie Brown," said Lucy.

Charlie Brown's ears perked up. Odds? What odds?

"One of these times I may not jerk the ball away," Lucy said.

"One of these times I may actually hold on to it."

"I never thought of it that way,"
Charlie Brown said.

Lucy kneeled on the ground and held the
football.

"Okay," Charlie Brown said.

"I'll come running up and kick it!"

Charlie Brown charged toward the ball.

"AAUGH!!"

Lucy grabbed the ball away—again!
WHAM!

"I'm sorry, Charlie Brown," Lucy said with a smile. "This wasn't the time!"

There would never *be* a next time, thought Charlie Brown.

But a few months later Charlie Brown saw Lucy holding the football for him to kick—again.

"She must think I'm really dumb," he said.

"Here we go, Charlie Brown," Lucy said.
"I will hold the ball and you run up
and kick it."

"No way," said Charlie Brown.

"What you really mean is that you will
pull the ball away and I'll land on my back
and kill myself."

"Never again," said Charlie Brown.

"Forget it!"

"Wait," said Lucy.

"I said, forget it," said Charlie Brown.
"I'm glad you are the only person who thinks I am dumb enough to fall for that trick again."

Charlie Brown walked away.

GOOD GRIEF!